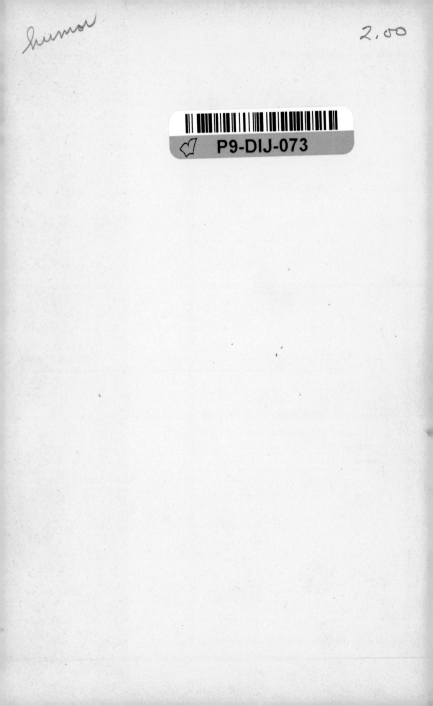

# Daily Except Sundays

OR, *What Every Commuter Should Know*

BY ED STREETER

*Illustrated by*

GLUYAS WILLIAMS

SIMON AND SCHUSTER · NEW YORK

*To*

**L. S.**

*Who Will Understand Why*

# Contents

Daily Except Sundays

# In Explanation

ALTHOUGH this is my first travel book I find tnat since 1921 I have covered 216,000 miles. That is more than nine times around the world! Figures like that stagger a man. They make fellows like Halliburton and Polo and Farson look like so many periwinkles.

Yet, curiously enough, I am not by nature a restless, adventure-seeking person. I have never had the slightest desire to sleep in a malaria-infested jungle or curl up on top of a glacier. On the contrary, I am generally regarded as a homebody.

The fact is that in my seventeen years of travel I have seldom been more than twenty-five miles from my house. I don't mind mileage but I do insist upon sleeping in my own bed every night, having a place to put old razor blades, and being able to lay my hand on a clean shirt in the morning. In short, I have solved the travel problem by being a commuter.

If anyone thinks that commuting is not traveling, let him try 5,400 trips between Fairview Manor and town—at his own expense, of course. I think he will find out very quickly that it is not just a question of being dragged back and forth like a tennis-court roller.

As a matter of fact, not everyone can be a good commuter. It calls for highly developed, special qualities—endurance, resourcefulness, decision, and cunning, tempered with a dash of ruthlessness. Hannibal, Livingstone, and Carrie Nation are types which give you an idea of what I mean.

It is a career that leaves its marks on those who follow it for long; you can easily pick an old commuter out of any crowd. His face has the alert, twitchy look of one whose life is spent matching wits with Time. His movements are quicker than most. He can make his way through a crowd like a snake through underbrush.

His eyes have a strained look at the corners from reading jiggling type. He never passes a clock without peering at it and is one of the few persons who can set his watch at a dogtrot without breaking his stride or the stem.

Almost invariably he carries a folded newspaper tucked under his right forearm. He uses this part of his body for a filing cabinet as naturally as a mother kangaroo uses her pouch. In fact, he is apt to keep his upper arm pressed tight against his ribs at all times even though there is nothing under it. This habit is so strong that we have seen a veteran commuter, when dining out, shake hands with his hostess and then look down quickly to see if he has dropped anything.

For my part, I lay no claim to these qualities, having been at this business for only seventeen years.

Compared to some of the grand old men of commuting, I am still a tyro. One need only refer to
such names as Stephen F. Guppy, fondly remem-
bered for forty-six years of travel between Boston
and Lowell on the B. & M., or to that veteran commuter C. E. Deeks who was recently given a testi-
monial dinner and a silver plaque by the New York,
New Haven, and Hartford Railroad to commemo-
rate fifty years of daily interchange between Bridgeport and New York.

Many commuters will remember with pride that
on this occasion Mr. Deeks' picture appeared in the
New York as well as the Bridgeport papers. Further-
more, Mr. Deeks, in his reply to the Assistant Vice-
President's address of presentation, recalled that,
since he had begun to use the road, its bonds had at
six different times been considered suitable investments for widows and orphans and at six other periods had been used by their owners to stuff cracks
in window frames.

Such men know the game and play it with high
idealism and courage. They have mastered com-
plexities and overcome hazards which few outsiders
know anything about. In fact, I myself did not realize what a technical thing commuting was until I
happened recently to have several talks on the subject with my friend and neighbor, Arthur Brophy.
Arthur and I see a great deal of each other as we

have missed the same train every morning for a number of years.

One day Arthur had the Big Idea. He said, "Look here, you're a writer. Why don't you write a book on this thing. Everyone's writing books about something."

It was nice of him to call me a writer as about all I have done in that line of any importance is the annual pamphlet for the Community Chest Drive. Travel books have had such a vogue, however, that it seemed like the obvious thing to do.

Then, after I actually began to write, I saw that it was going to be more than a travel book. I saw that it was going to have a Purpose. In fact, I decided to make it a guide—perhaps even an inspiration— for those thousands of young men and women who embark each year on a life of professional commuting pathetically ill equipped to cope with its dangers and pitfalls.

Cherishing this hope, therefore, I respectfully dedicate this book to George N. Klopper, our Divisional Traffic Agent, whom I have never met.

# Commuting
# Begins at Home

THE serious commuter starts his preparations the night before. As he snaps out the light he makes resolutions. Tomorrow the first whirr of the alarm clock will make him leap from his bed like a salmon. He will take up his morning exercises again. He will find time to fool with the children for a moment after breakfast. And, on top of all this, he will catch an earlier train. He will be at his desk to greet the boys, instead of hurrying past them, hoping they won't notice him.

All of which makes him feel proud and calm. He looks forward to the next day as a beautiful period of unhurried, efficient work. In five minutes he is snoring gently.

Obviously he has thrown himself into a vicious circle. Having gone to sleep in such a pleasant frame of mind he relaxes completely. By morning he will be completely anesthetized. He won't even hear the alarm clock when his wife turns it off. She will then call him as usual twenty minutes later.

The commuting mind works strangely at this hour of the morning. It is as uncontrollable as a puppy. There is no use reminding it of last night's resolutions. It won't understand. First it must spend several minutes studying the pattern of the sunlight

15

on the ceiling. Then it checks up the time available for dressing and eating. It reviews ten years of experience and finally decides that, by cutting corners here and there, the job can be done quicker on this particular morning. The time thus saved is spent in further study of the lights on the ceiling.

Don't try to control this process. It is wasted effort. The morning mind works that way. Nothing can be done about it.

.Then, mysteriously, something clicks. The feet shoot out from under the bedclothes. As they touch the cold floor the Commuter becomes a different man. He is now engaged in what is technically known as Working Up Tension.

His family flees discreetly at the sound of his pattering feet. For the next forty minutes they cease to be individuals. The world revolves around the Master. All effort is concentrated on getting him out of the house fully dressed, including hat, overcoat, briefcase (unopened), and the letters to be mailed in town. He must be assembled like a Ford, as he moves steadily from bed to train. Mistakes cannot be corrected. For he, like General Grant, cannot turn back.

To an outsider the scene might seem disordered. But an experienced Commuter has a time sense more accurate than a clock. We don't like to get mystic about it, but there it is.

*Then mysteriously something clicks*

If he misses the 8.16, the 8.24, and the 8.32, it is only because he subconsciously decided to do so before he rose. But strangely enough, he has never been known to miss the 8.44. That is the last commuting train from Fairview Manor.

His feet know to a split second when to explode from the covers. He refuses, or accepts, the second piece of toast instinctively. But the real time reservoir is the showerbath. Here is a sanctuary where one may meditate and hum resonantly on cold mornings while the inner clock ticks unheard. At just the proper moment it signals the right hand to turn on the cold. The hand obeys. The astonished bather is hit in the neck by an icy flood. He doesn't struggle. He is up against forces bigger than himself.

And now, shaved, dressed, and bathed, he enters the dining room. He is at his peak. The bread shoots into the toaster. The bell is rung. Loving hands push food before him. Others snatch the morning paper from Mother and prop it against the artificial fruit so that he who runs may read.

The orange juice is in. It's down. He crouches on the edge of his chair. His arms move with rhythmic swiftness. Bacon, eggs, toast, coffee. No jamming. No crowding. He is master of the situation. To Mother he recalls all the things she forgot to do yesterday. New items are added for her to forget today. He addresses the eggy little faces grouped

*He must be assembled like a Ford*

about him on the subject of their lousy school reports. He has come to the end of his patience. That's that.

A list of chores is outlined for the lout who comes once a week to do the outside. They are so complicated nobody understands. It doesn't matter. The climax is at hand. He looks at his watch. An unnecessary gesture. His inner clock has already sounded off. With a dramatic, hounded cry he rushes from the room, planting a flying kiss on his wife's forehead in the passing.

# Exodus

THERE are, of course, many different ways of getting from the home to the train. The trick is to choose *one*. Then stick to it. To vacillate is fatal. Space only permits us to touch on a few of the most popular methods.

### LIMOUSINE—CHAUFFEUR ATTACHED

Quick and impressive. Subject to sudden discontinuation, however, in bear markets. To be done properly involves smoking long, black cigar. Only very rich men can accomplish this, right after breakfast, without being sick. At least one double chin also advisable. Skinny men in rear seats of limousines are apt to give impression of having thumbed ride.

### WALKING

Healthful, at least in theory. Requires some experience in track work, both middle distances and sprints. Method largely confined to persons living in apartment houses a block from station. Anyone willing to commute fifty miles a day to sleep in an apartment house a block from the station should be watched carefully, but not imitated.

### BUS

Difficult and technical. No bus ever known to pass nearer than a quarter of a mile from house. This is a general rule which holds good regardless of loca-

*Skinny men are apt to give the impression of having thumbed a ride*

tion of house. Method should only be used by those able to do the 440 at reasonable speed without important aftereffects. Also, busses are always missed except in wet weather when one has to wait for them. A colorful and democratic means of transportation, but recommended only for younger men.

### SEDAN—WIFE ATTACHED

Gives good local impression. Daily evidence that things are hanging together. Much in vogue in one-car families. Works reasonably well in morning, barring fact that two people never finish breakfast at same time. Bad on return trip, however. Wife is either late at train causing husband to wait at station, or finds husband has missed train and goes home in huff. To be avoided, if possible, by all except stock brokers and others able to devote a large part of their afternoons to getting home. Important cause of American divorce.

### SEDAN—SOLO

This is the method which we favor personally. The only equipment necessary is a very old Ford. Ours was acquired for a bad debt. It was an even swap. There were times, at first, when we wished we had kept the debt. Gradually, however, it has grown like one of the family. Since the depression the resemblance gets stronger each year.

That car is almost human. It looks forward to its daily run to the station like an old hunter. When it feels someone crawling into it, its fenders shake with excitement. Once on the road, on a brisk fall morning, there's practically no controlling it. Its front wheels dash around like young bird dogs. They'll chase anything back and forth across the road from dead leaves to chipmunks. Sometimes they get going in different directions. Then there's nothing to do but stop everything and shake the wheel sternly until they come to heel.

Another thing about old cars like that is you don't notice the rattles. There are so many of them they blend. Single rattles drive us almost crazy. Get enough of them, though, and it's like living near Niagara Falls. After a while you don't hear the roar.

But I didn't mean to talk about my car. What we are studying here is the best way to catch the train. Which immediately raises the question—what train are you trying to catch? I am glad that came up, as it is one of the most important points in commuting. It is an issue which must be met squarely. Failure to do so in the early years of commuting is filling our asylums.

*Every commuter should have a regular train.* This is essential to an ordered life. Select one that will get you to the office earlier than necessary. Having done so make up your mind that you are going to miss it

*Causing husband to wait at the station*

regularly. Nothing is more demoralizing than to *catch* it one morning and *miss* it the next. It upsets your digestion and your stenographer. By having a regular train which you *never* catch, however, you will be leading an orderly existence and an independent life at the same time.

Personally, for example, our regular train is the 8.10. Up to date we have never had occasion to use it. It gives us a feeling of confidence, however, to have it in reserve.

Let's assume, now, that you have selected a regular train and relieved your local dealer of an old Ford. Don't feel that you can relax. You are still faced with technical and social problems. We have only time to touch on two by way of example.

What are you going to do about passing neighbors who are walking to the station?

Emphatically our advice is to pass them. In old Fords avoid all impulsive actions. They resent quick shuddering stops. Like airplanes, cars of this sort should be brought to rest in a long, graceful glide.

Besides, if you do a favor for fellows of this kind they will feel they have to be polite and amuse you. During the rest of the ride you will hear how bad their business is or how the country is going to hell. If you want to start the day crying, go ahead, but do it with your eyes open.

*Just as you come abreast make the car shy violently*

And in the end they will only hold you back. They don't know your routine. In that last exhilarating sprint between the parking space and the station they will be so much eel grass on your bottom. If, for example, you have missed the 8.10, your regular train, you probably have your mind on the 8.24. It's two to one that the 8.24 is *their* regular train. Naturally, they are in no hurry to catch it. The result is that the best of them will dawdle on you.

On the other hand, you don't want to appear rude. The safest way is to put on full speed whenever you see a familiar back. Just as you come abreast of it make the car shy violently as if it was dodging a nest of broken glass. The skill involved, if you want to keep from turning over, will give your face a strained, faraway look. Your friend will realize that you didn't see him and think no worse of you than he did before.

Approaching the station is a nervous moment for the novice. He must now come to grips with the unseen. Where is the train? Has it reached the bend by the brickyard? Is it at this moment creeping up to the station like a sneak thief? Is it already standing nervously beside the platform making those spasmodic, whirring noises under its cars? Is there plenty of time? Or is it necessary to go through a red light? Or, in God's name, what? Everything depends on the proper answers to these questions.

*Time, but full throttle necessary*

They say that an Indian could read his enemies' life secrets from a few broken twigs. Just so does the suburban world reveal itself to the trained commuter's eye. As he tops the hill near the station he has an unobstructed view for three blocks. Then a turn to the left and his goal is in sight. He appraises the situation somewhat as follows:

People walking. Time to spare.

Station bus coming in from Main Street. On the nose. A fine workmanlike job.

A number of people running. Time, but full throttle necessary.

Single person running. Possible if female. Improbable if male.

Empty street. Stop at corner and have shoes shined. Next train 8.32.

Through it all the commuter should bear in mind that it is essential for him to maintain an attitude of easy relaxation. This is important if he is to digest his breakfast and approach his work with the proper mental poise.

# Our Platform

WE CAN remember when people didn't "catch" trains. They "took" them.

In those days arriving at the station had some dignity to it. Traveling wasn't a lone wolf's job. When you went somewhere you took the whole family with you or else they all came down to see you off. In either event the entire works arrived at the trackside a good half hour before the show was scheduled to start. It wasn't such a good half hour either. The approved way of spending it was to stand in a circle, glowering at the suitcases, while the young fry leaned out over the edge of the platform or stuck hairpins in the gum machines.

Eventually the black monster came thundering in. Terrified passengers pressed back so that they wouldn't be sucked under the wheels. Everyone became suddenly animated. The knowledge that in another moment the dear one would be gone seemed to cheer them up. Good-bys were said all over again. The traveler promised everyone to take the greatest care of himself. He swore to write continuously. Then he hurried aboard so that he could look out of the window and wave.

The next few minutes were apt to be grisly, particularly if they were still loading baggage up forward. Those inside the car moved their lips. Those outside cupped their ears. The insiders tugged at the windows. Luckily they could never open them. Both sides made faces. Then, just as the whole thing became unbearable, the train started. Kisses were blown. Arms were swung. And at last it was gone, to the relief of everyone concerned.

What a change! When Mother takes Father to the station today she doesn't even come to a full stop. She hasn't time or the children will be late to school. As the car draws abreast of the station she merely shifts into low gear and dumps her man out like a mailbag.

It doesn't mean that Mother is turning into a cave woman. If she turns into anything it will be a hack driver. As it is she could give pointers to any professional on the stand.

Everything's changed. The train doesn't even thunder any more. It's electric. In the smarter suburban communities like Fairview Manor it slides in through a cut—like a snake in a ditch. From the street you can't even see if it's there. That's just to make it harder. It's the kind of thing that has done so much to put commuting on its present sporting basis.

Our trains started to come in through the drains about three years ago. In the old ground-level days they used to stop with the front car across Main Street. So many sedans ran into the side of them that

*The whole family came down to see you off*

it became too dangerous for the motorman. To overcome this they sank the whole thing.

We lost about as much as we gained. Formerly the fellows who lived on the south side of the tracks had to be across before the train arrived. Otherwise they were blocked. The only way they could get to the platform was to crawl under one of the cars. Obviously that's too messy, so there wasn't much to do when you were caught like that but to pound on the off doors and curse the brakemen until the train pulled out.

The game was played much more openly then. All trains used to toot just before they came round the bend. That was the signal for those who lived on the wrong side of the tracks to put their heads down and race for the crossing. The good ones could crouch as they came to the gates and go under them without missing a stride. And then, as the first car reached the crossing, it used to be a matter of civic pride to us to watch the last southsider come flying across its bows like a kangaroo.

That's all over. And, instead of us northsiders being able to leap from the running board of the sedan to the steps of the train like a steer thrower, we now have to go down a flight of concrete stairs. They are arranged so that a novice, rushing heedlessly down when there is no train in the station, will go flying across the platform and drop five feet to

*The next few minutes were apt to be grisly*

the tracks before he can stop. But this is no game
for novices.

As a gesture of safety they have put the paper boy
at the bottom of the stairs. He has his papers piled
on a bench in front of him. There are usually a
group of people shoving around trying to get a
paper, and if any amateur Israel Putnam comes
charging down the stairs he will hit this obstacle instead of plunging under the train.

If you arrive on the platform early, having just
missed a train let us say, you will find things quite
orderly. It is only just before the next train comes
in that buying a paper becomes a man's game. Then,
instead of handing your pennies to the boy you slap
them on the pile of papers. The player beside you
immediately tweaks the top paper from under them.
If the boy is quick he can grab a few in midair.
Otherwise they just roll around until that particular train is gone and things have settled down.

These are the preliminaries. The real fun begins
at the moment when the train arrives and the seasoned veterans begin to bound down the stairs four
abreast. The paper boy no longer tries to snatch
pennies. His energies are devoted to keeping his
feet. All thought of commercial gain has left him. It
is just a sporting struggle to prevent himself from
being swept onto the train with what is left of his
papers.

*There are usually a group of people shoving around*

The last few to come down don't even attempt to pay him. Bending, as they near the bottom, they grab a paper and disappear into the train like letters popping from a chute into a mailbag. The motormen are trained to stop so that there will be an open door opposite the stairs.

Those who still cherish a rag of the old Chesterfieldian spirit are apt to turn and wave at the paper boy, gasping "Tomorrow." The boy doesn't know, of course, whether they mean that they will pay him the next day or steal another paper at that time. It makes little difference. He doesn't know who they are, anyway. Besides, he is too busy trying to salvage his daily bread from the floor.

Up to date we have been discussing the man who *catches* the train. Obviously it is desirable either to catch it or miss it so completely that you are about in line for the next. No one can hope to do this every time, however. There is bound to come a day when you miss it by a whisker. That calls for the highest form of self-control and poise.

Suppose, for instance, that from across the plaza you see the last small group disappearing down the stairs. Manfully you prepare to achieve the impossible. Girding your loins, or buttoning your overcoat, as the case may be, you are off across the plaza in full cry. Horns squawk. Brakes squeal. Your ears ring with the curses of hacking mothers.

*They wave at the paper boy, gasping "Tomorrow"*

You take the stairs, two, three, four at a time. Only to find the doors shut against you. The train gives that peculiar, twitching motion that indicates it is about to start. From within a hundred sneering faces watch your failure.

The sap who missed the train! Missed it indeed! As if every one of the fools moving by you had not already missed some earlier train.

Such moments are given us to prove that Man is probably on a higher plane than the animals. Don't stand, half crouched, in front of them, looking like a trapped gorilla. Don't rush up and down, clawing and pounding at steel doors. Restrain yourself. When you shoot out on the platform and see that you are stymied, stop short like a polo pony. Turn quietly. Pay for your morning paper. Then sit down on the platform bench and light a cigarette. If your tongue is hanging out, open the paper and get behind it.

Show them that you are one who selects his trains.

*Show them that you are one who selects his trains*

# Friends,
# and How to Lose Them

I F YOU are accustomed to take one of those trains
that leave before eight o'clock, skip this chapter.
Your friends, if you have any, will be asleep at
home.

The only man we ever knew intimately who spe-
cialized in these 7 to 8 o'clock trains was a cotton
broker. The last train that would get him to his
office on time was the 8.24. For years he found it
practically impossible to catch, however. Each
morning he missed it by five or ten seconds. Finally
he hit on the expedient of calling it the 7.84. Since
that time he has had no difficulty, and on several occasions has found himself on the 8.15—to him the
7.75. On the other hand, the circumstances in this
case are so unusual that we do not feel he can be
considered a typical pre-eight commuter.

We stray from our subject, however. In this chapter we are to study the technique of losing friends.
But, you may say, this is not natural. People want
to make friends, not lose them. If one carries the
right quantity of the milk of human kindness he
will wish to mingle with his fellow men at this hour,
exchanging a cheery nod here, a handshake there,
choosing a pleasant companion for the townward
trip.

*Danger lurks on every side*

Perhaps that is what he *should* do. Forgive him, however, if he doesn't. Our commuter may be bloated with the milk of human kindness, but remember that from the time he reaches his office until he goes to bed fourteen hours later (if lucky), he is going to be milked vigorously and constantly.

In the monkey house Jocko may climb up on a shelf and enjoy an hour's uninterrupted meditation if he is in the mood. Movie stars have hide-outs in the Sierras. Even window dressers can sometimes pull down the shades. But the commuter knows no privacy in all his waking hours.

When the morning alarm clock jars him to consciousness his wife is beside him, ready to argue about shutting the window. During dressing and breakfast he must put joy and pep into a succession of sour little faces, reflecting unfinished homework. His business day must be spent trying to get something out of a lot of morons—or trying to prevent them from getting something out of him. His evening is, all too often, passed exchanging noises with comparative strangers when he would give a five-dollar bill to crawl under the piano and go to sleep beside the dog.

Only twice, in this unsolitary waste, can he be entirely alone. Once is on the train going to town in the morning. The other is on the train coming out

*He'll have you cutting your throat before you get to town*

at night. Small wonder if he treasures these interludes like pearls.

There is no moment in the day requiring more skillful handling than the brief period on the platform before the train rolls in. One false move, one sign of weakness, and he is ruined.

Danger lurks on every side. The President of the Citizens' League is a fine example of a confirmed lurker. His nature requires some human surface on which he can spread the gospel of civic reform. In his pocket he has complete figures on the cost of running your garbage district compared with that of all the other garbage districts in the county. What's more, you will have to read them, if he corners you, or else carry them around in your pocket all day. For, as he will point out, if he is going to spend his life trying to reduce your taxes the least fellows like you can do is to show a little interest.

Escape him and you are apt to find yourself surrounded by Parsons the stockbroker. He is prepared to furnish forty-five minutes' clean entertainment on the subject of Eureka Coppermines, with five years' earning figures, depletion reserves, and the details of the reorganization plan thrown in.

Coulter goes in for banks. His specialty is branches. His organization has 478 of them. At the moment he is revising and unifying forms. He has developed a new multiple form which will cut the

*There are obvious ways of dodging these people*

overhead down $17,462 per annum. If you are interested in this sort of thing the story of how it all happened is undoubtedly fascinating. On the other hand, you are still entitled to certain constitutional rights.

Then there is Schrambles. He is a professional pessimist. Things don't come bad enough for men like him. If the end of the world was announced he'd think up something worse for the next day.

Schrambles is a headline deducer. Give him a headline about a May dance of school children in Central Park, and he'll have you cutting your throat about the coming economic collapse before you get to town.

Klokenbush is funny. No one denies it, including Klokenbush. He always has a new story, sometimes ten or twelve. He's famous for the ones in Scotch dialect. They have two advantages. They are very long and nobody can understand what he's talking about. As a result it is not necessary to pay any attention. He will always indicate the place to laugh by becoming hysterical.

Of course there are obvious ways of dodging these people which suggest themselves immediately to the novice. A false beard and goggles, which could be removed when safely seated within the train. Covering the face with a newspaper or shawl. Hiding behind trunks. Such ruses, however, even though

*Dart quickly into the car behind*

effective might cause you to be considered eccentric or aloof. Nothing could be more damaging to your socioeconomic life.

A more subtle technique is called for. You must learn to lose your friends, but keep their friendship. It involves a cunning only to be acquired through experience. This is a book for beginners. We have included, therefore, only a few of the more elementary and basic principles.

1. When standing on the platform, talking to a friend, note carefully if he is smoking. If he is, walk forward toward the smoking cars with him. When you get there, say, "Well I see you're going to smoke, old man. Smoking cars always give me a headache in the morning." Then dart into the next car. Before he has realized what has happened you will have found a single seat and be safe.

2. Suppose, however, he is *not* smoking. Your problem is now harder. Take his arm and walk him to the nearest car door. *Be careful in doing so to keep him between you and the train.* This is most important. It is the only way you can have him in control at all times.

When opposite a car door push him gently in. Then step quickly aside allowing three or four passengers to crowd in between you. At this point shout to him, "Oh, are you going in there? I think I'll go up and smoke. See you later." By this time so many

*"I think I'll go up and smoke. See you later."*

people have jammed in behind him that he can't turn back and follow you.

3. There is a useful and interesting variant to this. If the usual crowd is milling round the door and you can't step aside, let your friend precede you. Then revolve your body counterclockwise, slowly but firmly. As a result you will find yourself presently on the outer edge of the group. It is then easy to pop silently into some other car.

Just before the end of the trip, if you want to curry a little favor, look him up and say "Well, what in the world became of you? I had a double seat and held it as long as I could, but you never showed up." This will make him feel that somehow he has been very stupid. He is apt to end by apologizing profusely.

4. On arriving at the platform it is a good precaution to join two men who are already talking together. Then, when the train arrives, all you have to do is drop back and let them worry about each other. If you feel any embarrassment about this, have an old letter handy in your pocket. You can excuse yourself at the last moment and drop it in the mailbox. The same letter can be used again and again for this purpose as the postman is almost sure to bring it back to your house.

Every commuter has a number of friends whom he has greeted cordially for years without the slight-

*You will be joined by some friend which will
involve an introduction*

est idea who they are. It is unwise to go up to one of these people when you find them standing alone on the platform. As sure as you do you will be joined by a third party which will involve an introduction. In such a case greet the newcomer cordially and say, "I'll have to leave you two fellows now. I forgot to mail a letter."

We remember one winter day when we were all standing around the stove in the waiting room and *two* of these unknown friends came up from different directions. The only thing we could do was to excuse ourselves politely and hide in the washroom until we heard the train come in.

Cold winter days present a particularly difficult problem. There is no chance to maneuver in a station waiting room. Besides, the air is usually so thick that you become groggy quickly and fall an easy victim to the first person to come along. The best solution is to have a heater in the automobile and sit there until the train arrives.

And now it appears around the bend. If you are experienced you will know to an inch where each car is destined to stop. If free, you will have taken up your position accordingly.

As the doors open a thin trickle of frightened-looking passengers try to get off. No one has ever learned who these people are or why they should be getting off at a suburban station when all normal

*No one has ever learned who these people are*

folk are going to town. They are outcasts among commuters and receive no consideration from the angry crowd, poised to rush in through the narrow doors. Whether they succeed in getting off, or are swept back into the train, we do not know as we always slide past them and are in the car while they are still struggling.

The double whistle has sounded. The doors are shut. The train picks up speed around the first bend. Lurching drunkenly, the parade of aisle walkers begins to file past. We're off!

# En Route

WE WOULD like to know more about these aisle walkers. As the train leaves each station a human chain staggers morosely through the cars. They press forward, each man's eyes fastened on the neck of the man ahead, and disappear into the next car.

A stranger might suppose that they were looking for a place to sit. But that can't be the answer, for they pass dozens of vacant seats without a sidelong glance. Where are they going? What do they seek? Is the lure of over-the-hill so strong that the next car forward beckons them forever on with a siren's empty promise? Is there a rainbow even on a commuting train?

It is the kind of thing that Sir James Barrie should have handled. It probably would have made him very happy to think of all those people walking through the train with fixed, unseeing eyes and finally stepping off the front end into the Never Never Land.

But we must leave these questions unanswered. Practical matters demand attention which concern us more than the daily fate of a few dozen commuters. The next forty-five minutes present pitfalls. Situations are about to arise. They must be dealt with in a vigorous, masterful way if we are to survive. We will take up the most important in this chapter.

### FRIENDS, AND HOW TO COMBAT THEM

Let us assume that you have entered the train with a friend. By great good luck all the double seats are taken. If you are behind him, the situation is easy to handle. Either drop into the nearest single seat, or, if you wish to do a more thorough job, duck out of sight for a moment on one of the end platforms, then turn and go in the opposite direction.

Once in front of him, however, you are obviously helpless. With an occasional gentle push between the shoulder blades he can keep you going until one of several things happen.

(*a*) You come to one of those uncomfortable, dark, little seats which run lengthwise at the ends of each car. If he wishes he can easily force you into it by twisting your shoulders slightly and pressing down at the same time. Thus you will find yourself jammed in the corner, head resting against the emergency toolbox. During the remainder of the trip you can amuse yourself, while he discourses, by shutting the sliding doors each time someone opens them—which is immediately after they are shut.

(*b*) He will insist on walking through fourteen cars until he finds a vacant seat for two right behind

*Where are they going? What do they seek?*

the motorman's cubbyhole. Your consolation will be that the trip is almost over.

(*c*) Having reached the front end of the front car it will be discovered that no double seats are left. By this time every seat behind will have been taken. Q.E.D.: You stand up all the way.

(*d*) Or finally, he may give out and suggest taking single aisle seats one in front of the other. By slipping into the seat behind he has you at his mercy. All he needs to do is to bend forward from the waist. He can then mumble in your ear, without fear of interruption, for forty-five minutes. Of course it is possible to avoid him by leaning forward also, but that would make the whole thing look like the start of a crew race, which would obviously be silly.

If you are sitting behind him, however, the situation is reversed. You are now in control. After a few words of polite conversation, merely lean back in the seat, snap the morning paper open in his face and enjoy complete privacy.

If the paper is held properly, he can neither peer over it or around it or signify his desire to communicate with you in any way except by tweaking its edge. Should he sink to this level merely peer around at him, nod, and say, "You bet." Then retire without further encouragement. Be careful not to lower the paper or let him push it aside. After a

*He can then mumble in your ear without fear of
interruption*

few attempts his inferiority complex will get the better of him and he will read his own paper—if he has one and can.

### HANDLING THE NEWSPAPER

The old-fashioned method of seizing a newspaper by its outside edges, and opening it in what is technically known as the full-arm-double-page-spread, went out of style with the advent of the modern, small apartment. After a few experiences with scraped knuckles and broken bric-a-brac people began to devise less painful and expensive ways of reading their papers. This led to what is now referred to as the Commuters' Fold.

One must not hope to attain proficiency in this art immediately. It may take months of practice during which you will get little from your morning paper but exercise. Once mastered, however, it would be a simple matter to read a modern forty-page newspaper in a drainpipe—discounting, of course, the poor lighting.

The technique is as follows. Fold the paper vertically down the middle. It is now reduced in size to the dimensions of a Chinese scroll.

Having read the first page you are now ready, presumably, to turn to the second. Fold the first page back on itself and seize the opposite folded edges by the thumb and forefinger of each hand. Turn.

*Merely peer around at him, nod, and say, "You bet"*

If you don't know what we are talking about at this point imagine how you will feel when you first try to do it. Remember, however, that men of even less mental capacity have mastered the trick.

On turning to page four fold the second sheet back on the first sheet. Repeat this process as you progress through the paper until one of the sheets is inadvertently folded in the wrong direction. The error will be detected immediately as the paper automatically locks itself and is converted into a kind of hollow cylinder or tube.

Once this has happened there is no use trying to undo the damage. Either stuff the whole thing under the seat or, if you must continue to read, seize it at the top and shake it until a few loose sheets detach themselves and fall to the floor. This should give you enough material to make thinking unnecessary until the station is reached.

There are still a few old-fashioned travelers, however, who cling stubbornly to the full-arm-double-page-spread. When seated beside one remember Napoleon's adage that "to become offensive is the best defense." Lean slightly away from your opponent and suddenly open the paper to its full width as if it were a skating sail. If this doesn't put a stop to the nuisance pretend to be looking for an item and run through the whole paper page by page flinging the arms wide at each opening.

GLUYAS
WILLIAMS

*Suddenly open the paper to its full width*

If this is done with sufficient spirit it will not only completely destroy the other fellow's paper but will probably knock his glasses off. You can then enjoy the remainder of the ride quietly while he paws helplessly for them on the floor.

Up to date we have referred only to flank attacks. The newspaper may also be used as an offensive weapon from the rear. When folded, as directed above, and held before the face, the top edge will droop like a reed and catch the person sitting in front of you in the back of his head just under his hat brim. As the eye travels down the column the hands are automatically raised, thus forcing the fellow's hat gradually over his nose.

The first three times this happens he will turn and glare. If the newspaper is skillfully handled, however, you will be hidden behind it. The fourth time he will shake it and say, "Willya-watchya paper." Hold the paper off to the side, look at it curiously, and remark, "Sorry." This treatment may be repeated as many times as appears desirable.

### ELBOW LOCKERS

Some people have a phobia about being in crowded elevators. Others become hysterical if they have to pass through narrow places. An elbow locker is one who becomes frantic if his elbows are not spread out, unfettered, like a buzzard's wings. Ob-

*Will catch the person in front just under his hat brim*

viously this is impractical in commuting car seats, which were tailored to fit two men sitting with folded arms.

Let us suppose that you are seated by the window, contentedly absorbing the day's news, when one of these creatures sinks into the seat beside you. Immediately your inside arm is pinioned to the back of the seat by a beefy elbow. Being a person of spirit, you retaliate instinctively by jerking it free and bringing it down smartly on top of his.

Once the game has started there is no stopping. It continues with increasing violence until one or the other is exhausted and allows his elbow to be permanently trapped—or the train arrives in town. In the latter event the one whose elbow is on top when the train stops is entitled to consider himself the winner.

It is difficult to combat an elbow pinioner except by force. Running through the paper full-arm-double-page-spread may confuse him. People like this are apt to retaliate in kind, however, which results in a shambles.

A ruse that is sometimes successful is to slouch into the corner, crossing the legs at the same time in such a manner as to wipe the boot on the offender's trouser leg. Then, when he leans forward to brush it off, you can lie down on the seat behind him. This

*Immediately your inside arm is pinioned*

is apt to produce high feeling and bad blood, however. It is not recommended.

### HOW TO BE POLITELY UNPLEASANT

Perfection is merely an ideal. Achilles had athlete's heel. Napoleon acted quite silly on his trip to Moscow. And so it is that even the wiliest commuter will occasionally fall into a trap.

Sooner or later, crowded against the window like a cornered panther, you will find yourself cut off from escape. Then you may well look out on the public dumping grounds, glittering in the sun, and realize that half your day's ration of privacy has been snatched away.

These are moments that call for the best in men. It is your duty not to give up without a fight. We are dealing here with a type which will increase in strength and boldness as you weaken. It is important to resist.

As the human pest beside you starts in on his hobby—as he will immediately—open your paper and start to read. Of course this is rude, but he expects it. It won't even slow him up.

Given luck, he may be a mild species—one who is not hardened by years of exposure. In such a case it will be found helpful to continue reading, shaking your head occasionally, and saying with a sigh, "I don't know. It's all too much for me." The paper should also be shaken at the same time to indicate that you have washed your hands of the whole problem and wish to devote yourself to the sport news.

The chances are that he will look at you in hurt astonishment for a few moments. Then he will try to crawl in between you and the paper with a new idea. Opening the paper suddenly in his face will break him of this in time.

But let us suppose that you are dealing with a more horny-skinned variety. This calls for sophisticated handling.

A basic rule is never to take your eyes from the paper. When a page must be turned, do it quickly, looking straight ahead. Suddenly start discussing the article you are reading. Your companion will continue his discourse on fish breeding or the stock market for a short while. Then, conscious of the sound of another human voice, he is apt to become puzzled and stop.

Experiment after a bit with short silences between your remarks. Don't become overconfident, however, and relapse entirely, once the ascendency has been gained.

If it confuses you to carry on a running comment while reading, give up trying to read the articles and just read the headlines aloud to him. In this way it is at least possible to run through the paper before arriving at the office.

To get the best results in either case, do not be bound by strict rules. Size up your man and act accordingly. If his sales resistance seems to be below par, select a long editorial, hand him the paper, and tell him to read it. Then take his paper or keep the sports section for yourself.

The chief difficulty is that people of this sort appear to have read all newspapers published in the English language before boarding the train. No one knows how they do it. Probably they get up an hour earlier than anyone else so that they may be free during this brief period to tell the world about fish breeding and their investments.

Although we never recommend sitting in front of two people who are talking, it is sometimes unavoidable. On such occasions you may have the good luck to sit in front of two bores who have accidentally cornered one another. This gives a splendid opportunity to study their methods.

The main thing to be noted is that neither one pays the slightest attention to the other. As a result their conversation will run something like this:

FIRST B: That Ritter Goldfields stock looks as if there might be something in it.

SECOND B (*absently*): I guess so. (*Brightening*) Say, Jack Hanforth told me a good one yesterday.

*Probably they get up an hour earlier than anyone else*

Know him? He works in that big textile house on
Mott Street. Know the one I mean? Oh, yes you do.
They almost went through the wringer in 1930.
My, I wish I could remember that name. You'd
know it if I said it. Well it doesn't matter anyway.
It seems there was an old Scotchman—You've heard
this, haven't you? Well this fellow used to get drunk
every Saturday night.—Say, stop me if you've heard
it. And one Saturday night Sandy went— (*Everyone
but the storyteller takes time out here to read the
paper.*)

FIRST B (*with a wistful expression*) : Yeah? That's
*good.* Say listen, I happen to know something about
this Ritter Goldfield situation. This is confidential,
of course. Last month their earnings increased
three hundred per cent. Have you got a piece of
paper? I want to show you."

But why go on? This sort of thing continues until
both become so irritated that they talk at the same
time or else they relapse into silence and do crossword puzzles.

### WINDOW OPENERS

There are few things more unpleasant than commuting beside an open window. Yet, from the time
the first crocus shows its head until the last leaf is
off the oak, the window openers are at work.

If you object to having your newspaper slatting back and forth in your face like a loose jib, if it annoys you to have your hat deposited in the seat behind and your glasses snapped into your lap each time you pass a train going in the opposite direction, if you are the kind of sissy who shuns the fresh tang of morning cinders against the skin—then avoid window openers.

But how? Sit on the aisle and your side partner will do the opening. Sit by the window and, standing on your foot and reaching across your helpless torso, he will tug at the window until you finally help him just to relieve the pain.

It is possible, with experience, to spot a chronic opener. For example, the following should be avoided down to ten degrees above zero:

(*a*)  High-school students.

(*b*)  Groups of little boys traveling from one station to the next. (Note: If the group consists of more than three it is best to leave the car entirely.)

(*c*)  Men wearing polo coats.

(*d*)  Men not wearing hats.

(*e*)  Fat men, particularly if they wear a handkerchief tucked under their collar.

(*f*)  Men chewing extinct cigars.

For the beginner, particularly during warm

weather, we recommend choosing an aisle seat next to a woman whenever possible.

Even then it is safer to select a woman with a semblance of a brim somewhere on her hat. There are many confirmed women window openers, but they will be found mostly in the turban group. Few, however, really attempt to do the job themselves. They will seize the little gadgets on either side of the window—those finger clips which have disfigured travelers' hands since the Civil War—and give one or two feminine tugs. After this they dust their hands together and look at you in a sweet, baffled way.

Courtesy now demands that you lift the hat (just why it is difficult to explain) and, leaning over her yielding form, you attempt to raise the window. Be careful not to try too hard in case it may be the one window on the train that opens easily. Merely seize the two gadgets, hold the breath, and make a face. This gives the impression of violent effort. She will be pleased and the window will remain closed.

Usually this ends it. Should she be insistent, however, pretend to slip and fall into her lap. This confuses her so that she will forget what started the commotion in the first place.

The trouble is that the man in the seat behind is apt to rise at this point. He raises *his* hat, and has a go at it, lying on his stomach across the seat back.

*Seize the two gadgets, hold the breath, and make a
face*

GWYAS
WILLIAMS

The odds are one to ten against him, however. If you see he is going to win all you have to do is to lift *your* hat once more, seize the opposite gadget, and press down.

The man in the seat in front may now get into the picture if your companion warrants it or if she is a very old lady who shouldn't have the window open anyway. You can double the odds against his accomplishing anything. His function is one of pure exhibitionism.

All three will then give you nasty looks, but you can afford to be generous with them, for you have assured yourself of a comfortable ride.

### SATURDAY-MORNING PROBLEMS

On this day all mothers who are raising their children along sound American lines take them into town to have their teeth straightened. Some day science will discover why the teeth of suburban children are sown like dragons'. Personally, we believe that it has something to do with the toast that is served at commuting breakfast tables. That is a subject, however, which is outside the scope of this book.

Whatever the cause may be, the commuter must be on the alert for mothers and their broods when he arrives at the station on Saturday morning.

Bear in mind that, as commuters, women are

GW

*The man in the seat in front may now get into the
picture*

most unprofessional. You can't nod them off. To the average woman a social event is a place where two or three find themselves gathered together, whether it be a station platform or an ice floe.

It is best, therefore, on Saturday morning, to stand behind the paper boy and do a little scouting before coming boldly into the open. If a brood is observed, milling aimlessly around its mother, go back to the upper level until the train comes in. Then it is easy to plunge down the steps at the last moment and into the smoker.

Once caught, however, there is no escape. You will have to walk through the whole train, if necessary, looking for two vacant seats. On Saturday morning you are apt to be out of luck, as the forward cars are usually half empty.

Now you will be required to turn over the back of a seat so that all may sit cozily facing each other. This is accomplished by locking the knees in a manner known to cabinet makers as dovetailing. Why anyone chooses to ride in this unpleasantly intimate way we cannot guess—but these are the facts.

You will be an immediate favorite with the children who know they won't get quite as much hell with a stranger around. If there are three of them, two will occupy the seat with you by popular vote. The youngest will sit with its mother so that it can put its white shoes on your lap.

*You will be an immediate favorite with the children*

During the first part of the trip your seat mates will kneel and look out of the window. Good breeding demands that the impulse to open it be resisted sternly. After they have thoroughly cleaned the soles of their boots on your trousers one at least will desire to stand in the aisle. The shift will be made across your body. Children are naturally brutal. The balance of the ride will be occupied in a hypocritical attempt to keep them from running out on the platform and falling off.

Until sufficient experience is gained to avoid a situation of this kind it is preferable to arise at dawn on Saturday morning and take the 7.20 or, even better, do not go in at all.

### THE TIMESAVER

About two minutes before the train arrives at its destination, the timesavers go into action. Springing up as a group, they push past every obstacle and rush to the end doors. There they stand, like old fire horses, waiting for their stalls to open.

They are quite harmless unless one of them happens to be sitting beside you and next to the window. They can be spotted quite easily. Usually they begin to get ready to save time about ten minutes before the train arrives. The paper is folded and placed under the arm. They run through their

*Towering above you, they glare down, silently
demanding passage*

pockets (probably a reflection on you). Finally they dust their knees and cough.

All this is the signal for rising. Towering above you they glare down, silently demanding passage. One may, of course, ignore them. In that event, however, they will either crawl over your knees as they would over a hedge fence or attempt to crash through them like underbrush.

Some people compromise by bending the knees outward so that there is just room to squeeze by. When the party is halfway through the opening it is then possible to suddenly crush him against the back of the seat ahead. This is an amusing experience. It is apt to end in a scene, however, and is not for beginners.

The most dignified solution is to step into the aisle, allowing the timesaver to pass unhindered. Then try to sneer at him as he passes in such a way as to indicate that you are relieved to be rid of him.

# Tickets
# and Their Takers

COMMUTING tickets have the same effect on us as bunkers. The more we concentrate on them the more trouble they cause. Just having to buy the miserable things every month is enough to ruin any disposition. It is like subscribing to the annual policemen's outing or paying the income tax, only twelve times a year instead of once.

If, for a lump sum, we could only be tattooed, or branded in some convenient place, and have done with the business forever! The monthly rate from Fairview Manor, for instance is $11.72. Just think of the things one could do with $11.72 each month. Like going to the theater. Or buying three bottles of Scotch. As a matter of fact, it would be more fun just to throw the money out the office window and watch people scramble for it.

Instead of that we have to hand it to a red-eyed ticket agent who isn't even glad to get it. And in return, at the end of the month, the railroad has taken us exactly nowhere. That's a high price to pay for staying in the same place.

To make matters worse we are charged each month for about twenty-five rides we never take. Not that we want to. It's the principle of the thing. Each ticket is good for sixty trips. No commuter living ever used as many as that. The highest we ever reached was forty-one.

Money isn't the worst part of this business, though. It's the actual *buying* of the ticket that makes commuters into old men. The first day of the month leaves scars on their souls. Any young man who has ambitions to commute should visit the station on one of these days and study the line which extends from the ticket window, once around the waiting room, out the side door and down the upper platform.

Those at the farthest end are sullen and resigned. The arrival and departure of a train arouses no spark of interest. They realize that many such must come and go before they even get within shooting distance of the ticket agent.

As one approaches the window, however, the atmosphere changes. There is hope in people's eyes. They become increasingly alert, until finally we reach the group at the head of the line, poised tense as whippets awaiting the gun.

Each one of these men has a gambling chance of making the next train, which is due in thirty seconds. If all they had to do was to step up to the window, pay their money, and get their ticket, the odds would be easy to calculate. Realizing this, however, the road has introduced a technique which makes it almost impossible to place a bet on which

*A convulsion runs down the line*

man will be left at the head of the line when the
next train pulls out.

The system works something like this. The first
man in line shoves $12 under the wicket. In return
the agent shoves out a ticket and a small pile of
nickels and pennies. Here comes the catch. The
ticket must be signed in two places by the purchaser.
On the window ledge is a single, crusted pen which
won't write, and a bottle containing a quarter inch
of melted tar or some similar gummy substance.

At this instant the agent announces in a disinter-
ested way: "Eight twenty-four coming in." A convulsion runs down the line like a snake hiccough-
ing. The first man crowds over to the edge of the
window as far as possible and starts to sign his name.
It is never Smith or Jones at a time like this, but
some polysyllabic affair like Pannamacoontz or Ga-
brilowitz. Those behind glare at him angrily.

After two or three dips into the bottle, during
which not so much as a scratch is made on the ticket,
the pen gives up and has a hemorrhage. The ticket
must now be pushed back to the agent who exam-
ines the two black puddles gloomily, and then gives
them a sharp blow with a limp piece of blotter, thus
spattering the signature in all directions. He finally
detaches the lower part carefully as if the whole
thing were a priceless work of art, and pushes the
ticket back.

*In winter it involved standing up and practically
getting undressed*

In the meanwhile the second and third men in line have both crowded in front of the tiny window and handed in their money at the same time. As a result the piles of change are hopelessly mixed up. Each grabs what appears to be a reasonable handful and addresses himself to signing.

The three lucky front men are now prepared to make a break for the train, which by all odds should have pulled out thirty seconds before. They find themselves ringed in by the waiting line. Hurling themselves against it they break through and are gone. No one knows if they catch the train—or cares. The tension in the waiting room relaxes. The 8.32 will not be due for eight minutes.

Of course one might avoid all this by buying the ticket before the first of the month. Somehow or other that is not good sportsmanship. It's like shooting wild ducks when they are sitting down, or riding ahead of the MFH. Once we bought ours a week early and then, on the last day of the old month, our wife sent it to the cleaners with a suit.

At least it might be supposed that, once having gone through an experience like this and bought the ticket, you could forget about it. That is just the trouble, however. One does. Where to carry the thing so that it won't be left on the bureau each day becomes the next major problem to be solved.

For many years we put ours in a billfold in our

*Of course one is apt to spill private papers all over the floor*

hip pocket. That worked all right as far as having it with us was concerned. But it raised other difficulties. Just as we were comfortably settled with our paper there was the ticket collector towering above us. And there we were sitting on our ticket like an optimistic hen.

It was bad enough trying to fish it out in warm weather. In winter, however, it involved standing up and practically getting undressed in the aisle. In crowded trains this was dangerous as lady standers were apt to assume you were an old-fashioned gentleman offering your seat, and slip into it while you were fumbling.

We tried carrying it inside our hat for a while. This was fairly satisfactory except that people frequently thought we were bowing when we took our hat off to get it. This involved an exchange of smiles and nods with absolute strangers. Also in summer the dye ran and gave us a peculiar rash on the forehead.

We now carry it in a wallet in the inside coat pocket. Of course, in pulling out a wallet one is apt to spill private papers all over the floor. Our experience is, however, that these papers, which we all carry about so carefully in our wallets, are usually without importance or meaning, anyway. We found that this was an excellent way to get rid of them.

In the old days there was some mental stimulation to be had in matching wits with the railroad. A commuter with a flair for logarithms could frequently work out ticket combinations which would lower the monthly costs considerably. As soon as the railroad found it out they changed the rules, of course, but it was fun while it lasted.

In those picturesque times, before the new flat rates were introduced, we had something to work on. Besides the monthly commuting tickets one could buy regular round-trippers, special round-trippers (which were only good on trains nobody wanted to take), ten-trippers, fifty-trippers, weeklies, and semimonthlies.

Old-timers will remember the summer of '26 when one J. Howard Wiltsbun of Fairview Manor, since deceased, discovered that, by buying a commutation ticket from town to Maplehurst, then paying cash from Maplehurst to Highridge, and finally using a fifty-tripper from Highridge to Fairview Manor, it was possible to save two cents a trip. This was probably the most brilliant combination ever worked out and caused the railroad no end of trouble.

No discussion of this subject would be complete without reference to the train crew—that mysterious body of men whose life is devoted to mutilating our tickets and taking them away as fast as we buy them.

Fifteen years of research have failed to produce any satisfactory data on these people. Their habits and customs remain as obscure as the day we moved to Fairview Manor. We can merely set down a few questions which bother us in the hope that someone more qualified will know the answer.

(1)   Where do train crews live? Does a member of a train crew get a house near his route or does he get a route near his house?

(2)   How do they get to work in the morning or home at night? Do their wives take them to the station like ordinary commuters? Do they meet them each night at some remote point at the end of the line?

(3)   What do train crews do between trips? Do they sit in their trains in the yards and play poker? Or do they go to the movies? We have never seen a train crew at the movies.

(4)   Why are some of these men labeled "Brakemen"? What do brakemen do? In the days when each car had hand brakes operated by a big iron wheel this was understandable. But now that the motorman stops the train, somehow or other, by blowing air on the wheels through a hose, the job of brakeman seems to us to be in the same class as a hansom-cab driver.

*The next one seems to grasp the point and says, "Six.
Three back. One gone down."*

(5) Why do motormen or engineers, or whatever they are called, wear overalls and a cloth cap with a balloon top? All they have to do is to sit in a little coop and twist a couple of handles. One might just as sensibly get into overalls and a cloth cap when about to drive a Ford.

(6) And why are these same motormen constantly buying great cans of coffee at the station lunch counter? No one else drinks coffee all day long like this. Why doesn't it give them the jitters?

(7) What do train crews talk about at stations? Each time the train comes to a stop they pop out from the doors like those Swiss figures that show whether it is stormy or fair outside. Their talk is as different from that of other men as their lives. One says, "Four on eighteen." The next one seems to grasp the point immediately and says, "Six. Three back. One gone down." A third nods and says, "Pick up from the end." In some countries talk of this kind would get men into serious trouble.

We regret most of all the passing of the conductor whom everyone knew. There used to be one on our line. His mustache and kind blue eyes were those of a retired colonel. Each morning he had a smile and a friendly nod for all the old-timers. He knew the names of each one, although none of them knew his.

It personalized things—made us feel that the road valued our trade.

But as the trains became more crowded he found it increasingly difficult to complete his rounds. Now he is gone—retired, we hope, to some sunny garden near a railroad track where he can watch the trains go by and be happy.

In his place we have a constantly changing stream of worried-looking men, shoving their way hurriedly through the cars so that they can finish before the train arrives in town. Our only thought is to keep them from snipping a hole through our forefinger as we push the ticket towards their clicking punch.

To them we are divided into two classes: things that have their tickets ready and things that have to fumble for them. To us they are so many dark blue vests that disturb us while we are reading the paper.

# Emergencies

ANYONE with flexible arteries and not handicapped by too much mentality can learn to commute. It requires a few years of apprenticeship, but so do the fine arts or plumbing. Given enough practice the average dodo can make the daily run without disgracing himself. The test comes, however, when something unusual happens. Let him strike a breakdown or a short circuit, let his seat companion pass out in his lap or his briefcase spring open as he rushes for a train and then he will have a chance to show his natural aptitude for the work.

How to act in such crises cannot be taught. Faced with a difficult situation the natural-born commuter draws on the great mystic forces within him. He does the right thing surely and instinctively. He evolves from the craftsman into the artist.

We have suggested below a few examples of commuting emergencies, not with the purpose of laying down rules, but to indicate pitfalls that lie in the path.

Those who say that commuting is dull speak without knowledge. Each train to town is the Bagdad Express. Adventure lurks around the corner. Time alone will teach the right grips to use in seizing it.

### THE BREAKDOWN

Breakdowns always occur (1) in the middle of large marshes, or (2) in areas devoted to the disposal

*It is then he has a chance to show his natural aptitude for the work*

of public waste. No one knows the reason for this, but experience proves it to be the case.

They are also most apt to occur on days when you haven't had time to buy a paper, or have been cornered by some notorious bore. The first intimation of crisis is when the train rolls to a dreamy stop. From the window nothing is to be seen, as far as the eye can reach, but the sparkle of tin cans. You are about to undergo your first breakdown.

At this point a pungent smell begins to filter through the floor of the car. It is as if a cheap cigar had come to rest on a horsehair sofa. A twitter of excitement arises. The brakeman enters. Everyone asks what is the matter. In haughty silence he passes out the other door.

People resume reading their morning papers. The human radio beside you turns itself on once more. Officials begin to gather beside the tracks and exchange dirty stories. The tin cans sparkle. All is as serene as in a London club.

After an hour spent in this pleasant manner the nomad spirit begins to reassert itself. Passengers begin to stir restlessly up and down the aisles. A few get off, form little groups beside the tracks, and also exchange dirty stories. An occasional brakeman is surrounded and captured. They remain loyal to the road, however, and refuse to talk.

Another half hour passes. During this period each

*Everyone asks what is the matter*

man watches his neighbor suspiciously. Then, as if at a signal, half the passengers rise and get off the train. The other half remain doggedly in their seats.

You must now decide with which group you are going to throw in your lot. First find out what your companion has in mind. If he decides to stay with the train, urge him to leave. Continue until you are sure he is adamant. Then rush away before he realizes what you are up to.

The morning air will be found bracing after the stuffy cars. You will be inclined to sneer at the faint-hearts who watch you from the windows as you slip, and slide on your back, down a muddy embankment. You are an action type. You go places.

At that moment the train, taking courage from your example, will start full speed ahead without warning. Your subsequent behavior depends, of course, on your temperament. If you are an old commuter you will have expected this and pay no attention, realizing that, had you stuck it out and remained motionless, the train would have done the same. The choice was yours, but you were predestined to lose either way.

Your strength should be saved for getting to the nearest highway. There you may be able to hire some conveyance to take you to town if you are an economic royalist—or at least to the nearest railway station where you can start life anew.

*From the window nothing is to be seen but the sparkle of tin cans*

Scattered along the road you will find little groups of your fellow travelers with the same idea in mind. Our only suggestion is that, if you have any money, either *walk* to the next town or thumb a ride from an old lady in a sedan. If you join one of the co-operative movements, with a roll in your pocket, the odds are that at the end of the trip you will pay ninety per cent of the bill. The others will pour pennies and nickels into your outstretched hands and leave, expressing the hope that they may see you again some time.

Another alternative is to phone your wife and have her drive you over to the golf club.

### SNOWSTORMS

Are you a lover of adventure? Then it is well, when choosing your home, to locate near a railroad which operates from a third rail. Such rails are notoriously temperamental. They will start a twelve-car train like a rocket, or reduce an elephant to a fine blue flame. Give them a half hour's treatment with snowflakes, on the other hand, and they fold up like a bridge table.

If the country in winter calls to your better nature —if you prefer to lie in bed rather than go to town— a third-rail line will be a great help. It is only necessary when you awake on a winter's morning to look at the porch roof. Should it show white don't bother

*He must resist the temptation to rush to the phone
every hour or so*

to get up. No trains will be running for hours. With a little luck and a northwest wind they may not run until spring.

Of course this works in reverse. If the snowstorm occurs while you are in town you cannot get home. This also has advantages. It gives you an opportunity to enjoy a quiet evening with old friends who also live on the line. Needless to say, the game should be played honorably. It is embarrassing, for example, to be detained in town by third-rail trouble and then discover later that your neighbors all arrived home at the usual hour.

The young commuter should remember, on nights like this, to telephone his family but once, and that early in the evening. Then he should be done with it. As his spirit grows expansive under the influence of pleasant companionship, he must resist the temptation to rush to the phone every hour or so and have a reassuring chat with the loved ones. There are times when they can be singularly unsympathetic with misfortune.

### HANDLING THE WEEK-END GUEST

At best, Monday morning is a dingy affair. Add a week-end guest or two and it is a complete eclipse. Not only must you buoy up your own flagging spirits. You must combat positive hysteria in these strangers whom you find under your roof.

*You will hear him dragging his bags down the stairs*

Even though they be seasoned commuters on their own line they will go all to bits when faced with catching a strange train. They have neither faith in themselves nor in your ability to lead them. Far easier to handle a group of nervous horses in a burning barn.

If your guest is a bachelor he will begin by getting up too early—which will probably be the first time in his life he has made this mistake. You will hear him dragging his bags down the stairs when you are still in bed. While dressing you can hear him opening and shutting the front door and pacing up and down the living room. By the time you come down he will have smoked himself into a palsy.

In honor of house guests your wife will, of course, insist on having griddle cakes and sausage for breakfast or some similar frippery. This will, of course, completely disorganize the kitchen. Hours will elapse before it can produce so much as a cup of coffee. Finally, when food does arrive, it is too late. Everyone takes a polite gulp and rushes for the automobile without bothering to say good-by to your wife or thank her for having reduced herself to a nervous wreck.

All the way to the station your guest will sit with his watch in his hand. Once there he becomes completely bewildered. Leave him, in order to buy the morning paper, and he is likely to disappear en-

*By rushing up and down the platform you will
probably find him*

tirely. By rushing up and down the platform you will probably find him, but then he will insist that he never moved, thus laying the blame entirely on you. About that time the train usually arrives, so there is no chance for a good quarrel.

The next complication will be caused by his baggage. Each seizes one of the small steamer trunks which he calls suitcases and staggers toward a door. Laden like pack mules, you will be the last ones in. This means that you can either stand up all the way, or walk forward four cars, holding the suitcase in front of you like a drum and beating it with your legs at each step.

If you should find a seat, without suffering anything more serious than housemaid's knee, one suitcase may be left in the aisle for new passengers to fall over. The other, with the pajama strings hanging out, should be shoved under your legs. This will cause you to sit with them sticking out straight like Mayor LaGuardia, which would be very comic if it didn't hurt so much. When the pain in your calves becomes unendurable there is nothing to do but offer your seat to a lady or draw your legs up under you for the rest of the trip like a Turk.

To avoid this painful procedure many hosts prefer to place their guest's suitcases on the entrance platform and sit on them without further struggle. Occasionally, if the commuter is a particularly ro-

*Occasionally he will succeed in buckling the thing into a shapeless mass*

bust person, he will succeed in buckling the thing into a shapeless mass during the course of the trip.

This only covers the case of a bachelor. Should your week-end guests consist of a married couple, the situation is well-nigh hopeless unless you are prepared to catch one of the late shopping trains. If you can't get rid of a combination like this on Sunday night the next best thing is to insist that the guest-wife stay over and have her breakfast in bed. This will enable her to spend the morning chatting with your own madam (who will have been up since dawn trying to introduce an atmosphere of quiet refinement into the chaos). Such a plan will drive the latter almost crazy. Someone must be sacrificed, however, and you have your living to make.

Failing in both these expedients, it is advisable to be called suddenly to a business conference in Washington on Sunday evening. You can then spend the night in a hotel in town. Thus, for a relatively small outlay, you will make your guests furiously jealous and be at the office before noon on Monday.

### WRONG TRAIN

This is the dread of every old commuter on the homeward journey. The longer he has been at it, the greater the danger. Suppose, for example, that for years you have been catching the 6 o'clock on track 10 or the 6.20 on track 18. Then, suddenly, the

*The brief moment of displeased silence tells him the worst*

railroad has one of those periods of whimsy when, for no good reason, the 6 o'clock is changed to track 7 and the 6.20 to track 12.

Mumbling to himself, the old commuter comes trotting across the waiting room with a glassy stare. Lost in introspection he dashes through familiar old gate 10. It clangs reassuringly on his coattails as it has for so many years. Finding a seat, he buries himself in his newspaper. Automatically he hands his ticket to the collector. The brief moment of displeased silence which follows tells him the worst. He is on the wrong train. It only remains to find out which one.

In such a situation it is important to keep absolutely quiet. Above everything do not make a scene. Commuters are a restless, sensation-loving people. Nothing interests them more than a man on a wrong train except perhaps one who has forgotten his ticket altogether and has no money.

If you give an instinctive cry of anguish, stamp your feet with frustration, or grapple with the collector, the entire car will turn and stare. Those farthest away will stand up so that they may see better. A certain proportion will continue to stare at you as if you were a leprechaun as long as you remain on the train.

Maintain your dignity. Merely incline the head slightly to indicate that you understand and that it is a matter of little moment where or in what direction you go. At the next station get off as if you were one of the boys. You can then decide whether to spend a month's pocket money on a taxi or wait for the next train back to town and start all over again.

In the latter event it is well to purchase a good book at the station newsstand and phone your wife that you have been detained in town on important business and will be out later in the evening.

The principal thing is never to admit to anyone that you took the wrong train.

### GOING PAST THE STATION

This is another commuter's nightmare. It never happens unless you are expecting guests to dinner or on particularly stormy nights when the little woman is shivering angrily in the car, cursing you for not being rich enough to own a chauffeur.

In either event there is only one course open. Go on to the next station. Grab a taxi and drive hell-for-leather back to the point where you should have debarked in the first place. If, on arrival, you are lucky enough to meet another train just pulling in, you can, of course, mingle with the passengers and say that you were held up by a conference and missed your train.

Such luck is rare, however. Ten to one there will be no one moving in front of the waiting row of taxis and cars but a few little boys selling the *Saturday Evening Post*. At this point there are several choices of action open. If the next train is due in a few minutes, hide in the baggage room. When it arrives merge with the passengers and announce yourself as above.

Or you may take a wide detour through the darkness, creep up on your car from behind and say that a friend living farther down the line drove you out. By popping up in a jolly, playful  sort of way you are apt to startle your wife so that she will not ask any further questions. In fact, if done well, she may not speak for the rest of the evening.

Should you feel particularly sure of yourself you may rush at the car from the front, exclaiming crossly, "Well, well, darling, where have you been hiding? I've been hunting for you ever since the last train got in." Obviously this is unwise if she meets you at the same spot each evening, or if there are only two or three cars in sight.

### LEAVING SUITCASE ON TRAIN

This is a particular pitfall for *young* commuters. They fail to realize, until experience teaches otherwise, that a commuter's natural state is one of semi-consciousness. Like an actor, letter-perfect in his part, he is completely confused by any deviation from routine.

*Creep up on your car from behind in a jolly, playful*
*sort of way*

GLUYAS
WILLIAMS

For example, at the end of every car, there are two little seats running parallel to the aisle. Between these and the cross seats is what appears to be a handy place for baggage. It is a trap, a snare set for the uninitiated. No matter how fine a mind a person may have, if he leaves his suitcase in one of these places and takes a seat elsewhere he will eventually have the thrill of standing on the home platform and watching the train pull out with all his worldly goods still aboard.

There are only two sensible things to do in such a situation. The first is to let the thing go and pretend it was stolen. This is by far the best plan, but beyond the means of most commuters.

The second is to go home quietly. On arrival, phone the station at the end of the line. By doing so you will establish the fact that the-man-who-has-the-key-to-the-room-in-which-your-bag-may-or-may-not-be has gone home to supper. He will be back in an hour. This is routine and a matter of railroad tradition.

And so, having eaten your own meal, you pile the family into the car and drive to the end of the line. The man has returned from his supper and gone out again. He will be back in an hour. You wait. He returns in an hour and a half. Your bag has been sent back to the city. It can be had, upon proper identification, at the Lost and Found Department,

*Watching the train pull out with all his worldly goods still aboard*

Room 4217-A. The drive home is made in silence.

The next night, if you are keen enough to find Room 4217-A and locate your property, the whole experience may be repeated. We know of one commuter who did this three times before he succeeded in getting his bag back to his home.

Old-timers do not have this trouble. Realizing their mental condition, they never let a suitcase out of their sight. As a further safeguard they place it so that they cannot leave their seat without falling over it. It is true that there are cases on record of commuters who have fallen over their suitcase, picked themselves up, and left it lying in the aisle. These were *very* old-timers, however, and their experience is unusual.

### THE DEMON RUM

Personally, we enjoy gaiety and like everyone to have a good time. We may have faults, but narrow-mindedness is not one of them. Tastes differ, of course. We realize that. And if a commuter wants to stand at the end of the car and bellow at his fellow passengers all the way home, that's O.K. with us—as long as he stays at the end of the car.

When confronted with one of these traveling Falstaffs, the principal thing to remember is never to catch his eye. If you must see the fun, peek around the edge of your paper or punch a hole through it

*The-man-who etc. has returned from his supper and gone out again. You wait*

with your finger. Be prepared to retire like a turtle if he so much as glances in your direction. It is best not to look at all, however. If you do there is sure to come a time when you are not quick enough and contact will be made.

With a fixed, glassy stare he creeps towards you. On the way he makes running comments about your hat, your glasses, and the shape of your nose. Delighted fellow passengers lean out into the aisles. You can hear their approving laughter as the attacker gives a final summing up of your character.

Now he is standing at your side, explaining to the gentleman across the aisle why he doesn't like you. Even this is preferable to the second stage of warm friendliness which follows. It begins when he feels the need of something to lean on. With his arms around your neck he lies affectionately on your shoulder until the next curve, when he rolls into your lap.

Through it all you must not show annoyance. It is very un-American to be cross with a train drunk. As your newspaper is crumpled into a ball, smile. As your glasses tinkle to the floor, pat him on the back. When your hat is pulled down over your nose, join the car in hearty laughter. If you can convince him that you are a Good Sport he will become bored with you and go to sleep. If you don't convince him—God help you.

*On the way he makes running comments about your
hat, your glasses, and the shape of your nose*

On Christmas and New Year's Eve it is well to wear old clothes to town. For on those days the spirit of carnival gets into most of the passengers about two hours before catching the train. Fortunately most of them get seats and go to sleep immediately. The worst they can do then is to lean against you and snore.

The ones who come in too late for a seat should be watched carefully. They usually travel in groups and are full of what appears at first glance to be fun. This starts with loud laughter and develops into a pushing game which continues until a goal is made by all the players falling into your lap.

An excellent antidote on these occasions is to have five or six Manhattans in quick succession just before boarding the train. Arrive early enough to get an inside seat. Pin a note on the lapel of your overcoat, stating the name of your station. You will have a restful and refreshing trip.

### THE LITTLE WOMAN IS LATE

There is no time of the day when a man feels sorrier for himself than upon arriving home at night. The station plaza is filled with cars, glistening under the arc lights. Smiling faces peer at him from sedan windows. There is a gaiety about it all that is out of tune with his mood.

Morose thoughts come to the surface of our consciousness at such moments. What have those smiling faces been doing all day while we were sharpen-
ing our noses on the grindstone? Lunching together
at the club, perhaps? An afternoon of bridge? The
movies possibly? A friend's for tea?

The fact that they have spent the period rushing
from the A. & P. to Sam Lee, the Chinese launderer,
hacking children back and forth to school, getting a
new dog license and putting shelf paper in the linen
closet, has nothing to do with the case. We are tired.
If we want to be hurt and morose who has a better
right?

And so, looking out on this frivolous scene, we
derive a certain grim pleasure from thinking of those
Mexican horses who, hitched to a pole and blind-
folded, walk round and round a millstone all day.

The familiar red sedan with the bent front fender
is nowhere to be seen. Other cars fill up and drive
away. We are left alone. The grim thoughts now
enter in a body and stage a sit-down strike. It was
with great difficulty that we finished our work at the
office in order to catch this train. (We spent the last
half hour there talking to Brown about his arthri-
tis.) We had planned this brief period before dinner so that we might be with the children. (We
know perfectly well that the Hendersons asked us

for cocktails.) Undoubtedly she is sitting in some gay group, talking and laughing, forgetful of our very existence.

And now, when things are at their blackest, the little woman, having prepared the youngest children's spinach, forced it down their throats with the handle of a knife, sorted the laundry, put it away, and called for our dress pants at the tailor's, comes skidding into the plaza.

We are face to face with our greatest test of character. If we can smile at times like these—why then we are men indeed, my boy.

### THEATER TRAINS

Some people, who live in the city, may wonder why we include this subject in a chapter on emergencies. Anyone who has ever spent an hour after the theater sitting in a cold station in evening clothes, or who, on arriving home, has walked three blocks through ankle-deep slush to the parking place, knows that theater trains are nothing but a succession of emergencies.

Our only advice on this subject is:

      (*a*)  Drive to town in the car.

      (*b*)  Stay in town all night.

      (*c*)  Give up the theater.

# Eventide

THE day is over. The commuters converge on the stations like black ants. The evening rush for the home fires has begun. Strangely enough, however, it is as different from the morning in-trek as a shower bath is from a hot tub.

Work-weary, the commuter has shed all those illusions which so persistently arise in man with each new dawn. Life has made him a realist—as wily and cunning as any beast of the forest. The forty-five minutes of privacy which may be his with care have become doubly precious with the passing hours. He is prepared to fight for them.

There are new and different rules to be observed. He knows them. He knows that each one must be obeyed.

The train stands guilelessly beside the platform. Like a purring cat it sends out an occasional wham-wham-wham from beneath its cars. He approaches it—but only after looking carefully through each window. This is most important. It is Rule One, for it gives him a chance to observe the occupants of each car before entering.

He selects a car, apparently populated by strangers, and enters—from the rear. This is also important. Obviously to enter from the front would involve walking through the car facing the passengers. No matter how carefully the preliminary reconnaissance has been made, Parsons, Coulter, or Schrambles may be sitting there, patting the empty seat beside them encouragingly as if they expected you to jump up on it and lick their faces.

By entering from the rear, however, one has a second chance to look over the ground before making some irretrievable mistake. Just as an experienced eye can recognize the make of an automobile from the back, so can a practiced commuter recognize a familiar old hat or pair of ears at a car's length.

One more point. Having taken all these precautions it is always best to enter a car with a light tread. Even though the field seems surely clear there is no need to take unnecessary chances. The steel platform of a modern car is so constructed that, when stepped on with a full confident stride, it gives out a harsh clang of warning, like the doorbell of a French shop. Invariably ten per cent of those seated in the car will turn around. Obviously, there may be a friend among them. Your clever commuter, therefore, creeps onto the platform with the soft-toed stealth of a panther.

Having made his approach unobserved; having assured himself by double inspection that he has never seen one of the passengers before in his life, he must now choose a desirable seat before actually entering the car.

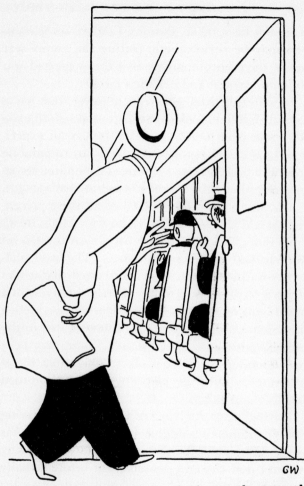

*One has a second chance to look over the ground*

There are three important points to be considered in this connection:

(1) It should be a seat already occupied by one passenger. Should he choose an empty seat, all his precautions may have been in vain. Sitting with an open seat beside him, he will fall victim to the first public menace who walks down the aisle.

(2) The seat behind should also be occupied by a *single* passenger. Leave an empty double seat in the rear and two women friends are sure to come along and sit there. Anyone who has ever sat in front of two women friends who have spent the afternoon shopping (and they always have) knows what a harrowing experience it can be.

The discussion of their individual wardrobes will not only preclude any possibility of reading the paper, but in some temperaments the sound of it produces a form of temporary madness which may last all evening.

It is a good rule never to sit in front of two people unless you have had them under observation long enough to be sure that they are total strangers. Even then you may be fooled. They will frequently sit in moody silence until you are settled down and the car is full. Then they will break into a torrent of words.

This is more apt to be the case with two men

sitting together than with two women or a man and
a woman. Two women friends are easily spotted as
they both talk continuously. A man and woman will
usually talk (or at least the woman will) until the
train reaches the first station. After that the man
becomes sulky and reads his newspaper. The woman
will talk for two or three stations more, then give it
up and either pretend to read over the man's shoulder or look out the window.

(3) It is important to select a seat partner so
built that he or she takes up the minimum amount
of seat room. In this way you acquire the maximum
amount for yourself. With a little practice one can
become amazingly accurate in estimating the dimensions of that portion of the passenger's torso which
is concealed from view below the seat back.

The same principles are used as in estimating the
roots of trees. Just as the branches of an apple tree,
for example, indicate the spread of its roots, so may
the breadth of the human shoulder be used for similar computations.

Select a pair of narrow shoulders supporting a
thin, scrawny neck and you will be reasonably assured of a comfortable trip. If possible choose a man.
For some reason or other they run more true to type.
Beware particularly of women with narrow and
*steeply sloping* shoulders. They are apt to belong to

what is known as the pyramidal type. That is to say, they are built like the pyramids and are about as uncomfortable to sit beside.

(4) Whenever possible select a seat that is *behind* one already occupied by a single passenger. This is only important when there is a circus or rodeo in town. The most dreadful thing that can happen to a tired man is to sit behind a tired woman with two children who have just been to a circus or a rodeo.

It is a known medical fact that young children who have been thus overstimulated are unable to sit quietly. Something in their nature, it appears, forces them to kneel on the seat facing backward. That, of course, means facing you. Invariably they carry whips and balloons. Why children should be given whips and balloons because they have seen a circus or rodeo is something we leave to the sociologists. Certainly it should not be allowed unless the other passengers are given a chance to arm themselves in like manner.

However that may be, there they are. And if you have been so clumsy as to let yourself in for something of this kind the wisest thing you can do is to go out and stand on the platform. Otherwise you will feel you have been playing the lead part in *Uncle Tom's Cabin* before you reach home.

(5) If you have arrived at the train three or four

*Invariably they carry whips and balloons*

minutes early and are obliged to take an empty seat
you are in a vulnerable position as we have pointed
out above. It may be possible to save yourself, however, by opening your newspaper full width and
crouching behind it as if it were a duck blind.

Should your arms be strong enough to hold this
position until some stranger sinks into the seat beside you, you are safe. Even then it is best not to look
at him. If it should be Parsons or Coulter or Schrambles there is just one chance in a hundred that if you
don't startle him with some sudden motion he
will not detect your presence for at least a few
stations.

We have assumed a dignified arrival at the station
with ample time to choose a seat. This is obviously
academic. More often it is our destiny to swing onto
the last car and face the prospect of standing most
of the trip.

Even though the aisles are jammed, however,
hope dies hard. Through car after car we push our
way over a hundred pairs of cringing feet. It is only
when we reach the head car, jammed to the doors
with die-hards like ourselves, that we admit defeat.

Almost invariably this happens on evenings when
we are bearing home an armful of odds and ends; a
couple of books from the lending library, a briefcase
full of office papers, a magazine sent to us under the

*You may now try to read your newspaper*

illusion that some day our company would advertise in it, a big box of something that our wife had delivered at the office, and, of course, the evening paper.

Now, after a few years of commuting, one doesn't mind these little things if they can be placed in the lap and forgotten. But when it comes to juggling them for forty-five minutes in a crowded aisle that's something else.

The books and magazine can be placed underneath each arm and held there by sheer pressure. The box can go on the floor between the legs. If you are young and optimistic you may now try to read your newspaper. This project will last until the first curve. At that point you will automatically release the two books and the magazine, put your foot on the box, and fall across the shoulders of the nearest seated passenger.

Such goings-on are, of course, mutually undesirable. After one or two experiences you will merely cling grimly to the nearest seat back and resolve to miss your trains more thoroughly in the future.

We had a friend once who, whenever he was forced to stand, used to take up a position by the water cooler and wait for the first station. Then he would shout out the name of some station near the end of the line. Invariably a few people would wake up from a sound sleep with a startled cry and stagger from the train. In this unscrupulous manner he always found a seat.

There is no quarter on these trains. Each one lives by his wits. Women share an equality with men beyond their fondest dreams of twenty years ago. As my friend Arthur Brophy often says, "Let them stand. They can sit on juries."

The day's work is over. The roaring pavements lie behind. The molten sun sinks to rest behind a row of billboards. Somewhere, presumably, lowing kine wind slowly o'er the lea. No further effort is expected of us—at least until we get home. The next forty-five minutes are ours to do with as we will.

The evening paper palls. The only thing that keeps it from being yesterday's is the date. The market is strong except for our stocks which are all down a half. All over the world, people are busily engaged in annihilating one another. Politicians continue to be dumb, statesmen incomprehensible. Policemen shoot thugs. Thugs shoot policemen. Elmer Ramsbottom, thirteen, P. S. No. 44, wins another prize with his airplane model.

All these things belong outside of our world. The brakeman puts his head in the door. He says something that sounds like "Ellumhoist." People get off.

Rows of little houses all alike. Rows of dusty little trees. Add some pools of rain water. Garnish with tin cans and serve.

Half a dozen commuters take a short cut up the embankment. One holds up the top wire while the others crawl through.

More rows of little houses. Vacant lots. Weeds. Rusty auto bodies. Public dumps. Private dumps. A vacant factory. Nature is wonderful, but it bores us.

A few seats down we see our old friend Mallory. Good old Mallory! We haven't seen him for a long time. He hasn't noticed us. We will go and sit with him when we get to Sky Gardens which is only one station from Fairview Manor. Perhaps.

We watch our fellow passengers with languid interest. What do they do on trains, these strangers who have traveled with us so intimately and so long. As nearly as we can figure it out, without exerting ourselves too much, they divide themselves into seven major groups:

(*a*) Newspaper readers; (*b*) crossword puzzlers; (*c*) magazine and book readers; (*d*) cardplayers; (*e*) card watchers; (*f*) starers, and (*g*) sleepers.

The last three might be merged, as it takes close observation to distinguish one from another.

Group *b* is by far the most approachable. Groups *a* and *c* are privacy lovers. They should only be interrupted in emergencies and then only if they appear to be hurt.

For sheer concentration, however, the cardplayers lead the field. They are at it every night, the same faces. No matter how early one arrives at the train they are in their usual places, newspapers across their knees, dealing the cards. The only way we can explain it is that maybe they don't get off the train in the morning but play all day in the yards.

Around them are grouped the watchers. Their eyes never leave the cards, yet their faces are those of men who are far away. A good card watcher will gladly stand lurching in the aisle for an hour rather than miss a single trick.

The cardplayers become most interesting when they reach their station. Here we find no restless commuters, waiting to rush off the train before the wheels stop turning. The train crews know their habits and act accordingly.

As the train slows down for their station the brakeman sticks his head into the group and bellows the name. No one pays any attention.

The train stops. Passengers file off. The players play on. Again the brakeman calls out the name of the station, his hand on the signal cord. One of the players is apt to look up at this point, nod, and say, "Coming, George. Hold it."

Then very deliberately they finish the trick, fold

the newspapers, put away the cards, and leave the train.

On at least one occasion they have been known to remove the newspapers and cards intact to the platform and finish out the hand at the bottom of the steps. On these occasions they are followed, of course, by the card watchers who never relax their vigil until they have seen the cards put away.

Our eyes turn drowsily to the car ads—parallel galleries of feminine charm. They look so happy and innocent, these young girls. Yet he who reads must realize what dangerous lives they lead. Only by the constant application, both inside and out, of carloads of drugs do they escape receding gums, sour stomach, morning mouth, bad complexions, athlete's foot, dandruff, yellow teeth, and numerous other undignified complaints.

It all strikes us as slightly indelicate. We wonder if Browning and Shelley and all those fellows would have written as they did had they known these things about women. It isn't quite cricket—like tipping off a little child on Santa Claus. We resent it. The world is not all beauty. But why must every member of the Manufacturers' Association spend his stockholders' money to tell us about it.

Undoubtedly an occasional cockroach crawls across the Mona Lisa. It would not surprise us if there were rats in the Taj Mahal. We have forgotten

*No one cares, least of all the sleeper*

what the base of perfume is, but have a dim idea it's something terrible. And so what?

The question interests us. We close our eyes, the better to consider it. Our head rests against the window. This involves removing the hat. From our lap it slides unnoticed to the floor. So does the evening paper. Strange as it may sound to a noncommuter, we sleep. Does the head droop? Does the lower jaw unhinge? No one cares, least of all the sleeper.

Fairview Manor! The familiar sound is like a bugle to a war horse. Gathering our hat and paper, we stagger to the platform. A hasty glance around to make sure it is the right station. Yes, there are the rows of posters on which the mustache and goatee artists have worked so patiently. Scribbled on the walls are the familiar slogans: "Frank is a nut"; "Minny loves Walter"; and "Frank M. Zabriskie, 427 Leander Avenue, Halifax, N. S." The last, in indelible ink, has been there for years. We have often felt like writing him. And here are the ten little boys trying to sell the local paper and the *Saturday Evening Post*. Daily they have screamed with vain hope at each arriving train.

It is the same station we left hours before. And yet it would not be true to call it that. For it is not the same at all. It is as different as New York and Vladivostok. Even the people who move so slowly

*Automobiles are milling about the plaza*

up the steps, discussing the market and arranging bridge games, are different.

Automobiles are milling about the plaza like sampans on the Yangtze-Poo. Little women, sighting their men, lean hopefully on the horn. Chauffeurs, under better emotional control, stare moodily. Commuters, failing to locate their loved ones, stand glowering under the station eaves.

We wind our way through the traffic toward the parking space. Only a few hours before we covered this ground in ten flat. The little old Ford stands patiently where it rolled to rest—and rust. We could almost believe that its differential wagged slightly as we approached. It starts with a roar and fairly leaps out of the graveled enclosure.

Home to the little ones. Home! The word thrills us with its deep significance. They are grouped tensely round the radio. We enter to the sound of galloping hooves. "Get that yellow cur," cries a fine baritone voice. Two pistol shots ring out. We announce ourselves with a cheery shout. From our point of view the scene calls for tossing a baby at this point.

Our little circle greets us with angry frowns. "For heaven's sake, Dad, keep quiet. Mysterious Drummond is on."

We become ourselves. We relax.